MAR 2002

LI

PARTS

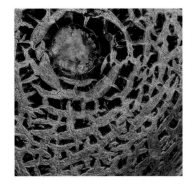

PARTS

Shelley Rotner

Walker & Company
New York

Petals on top,
leaves down below

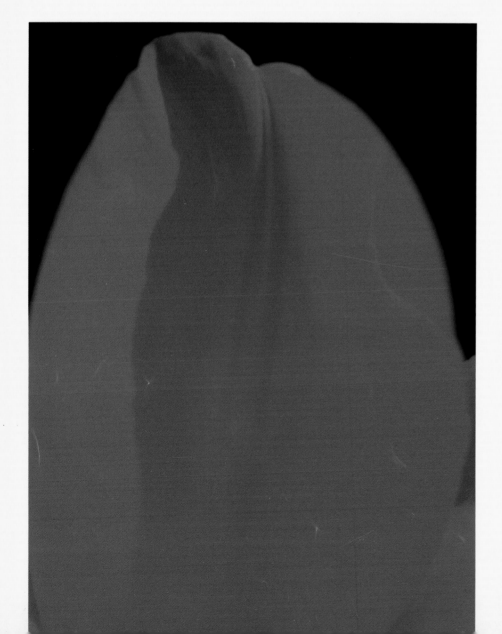

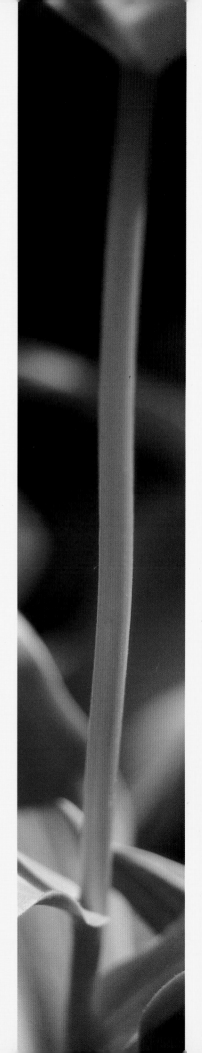

Up out of the ground
they grow

On tall green
stems stand bright
red towers

Come
and smell
the pretty
FLOWERS.

What's bright yellow, with seats in rows

Up and down the streets it goes

Red lights flash
when it stops for us

Climb on board the big
SCHOOL BUS.

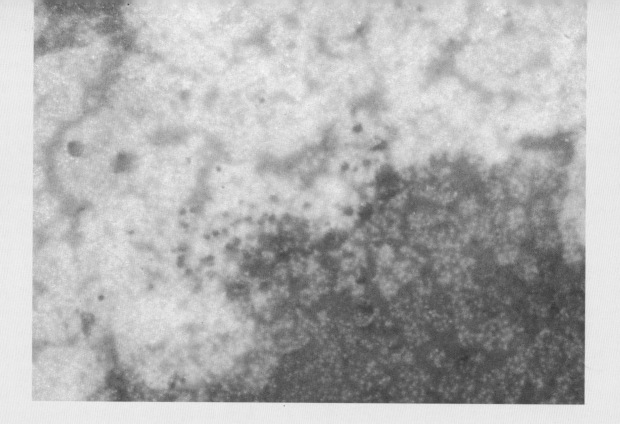

Smooth and round
with a striped green skin

Red fruit,
black seeds hidden within

Garden ripe and
ready to eat

Taste the
WATERMELON,
juicy and sweet.

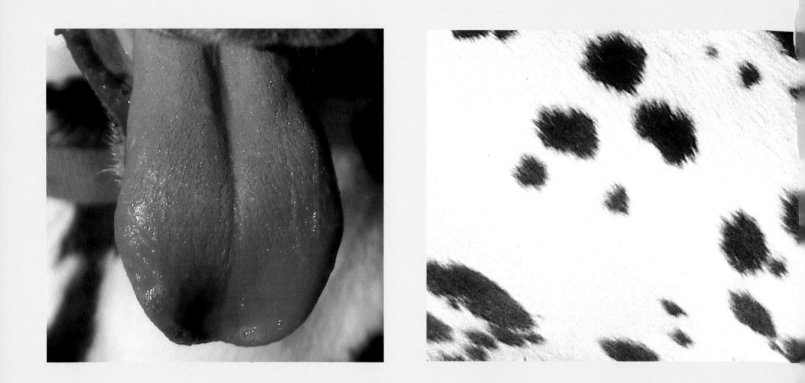

A tongue to lick, a tail to wag

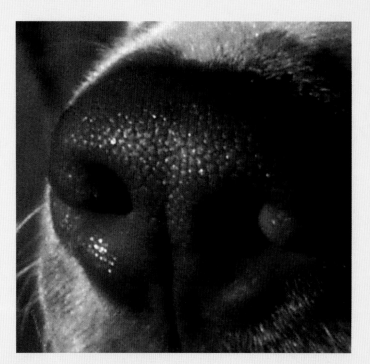

Around his neck he wears a tag

His fur is soft,
his nose is wet

A loyal
DOG
is one great pet.

Pedal hard, switch the gears

Going fast, have no fears

Ride around without a care

Your BICYCLE takes you anywhere.

Climb up the steps, one, two, three, four

Stand on the porch, knock on the door

I always return after I roam

To the place where I live—
my house,
my HOME.

A head
on top

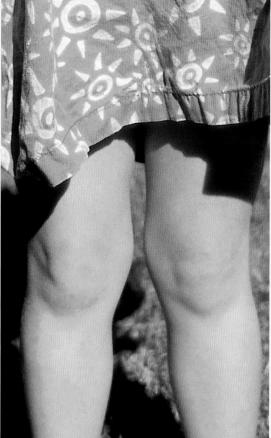

and legs
below

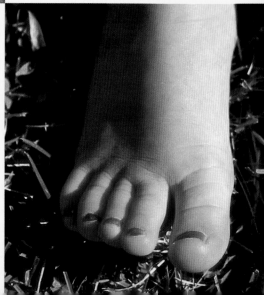

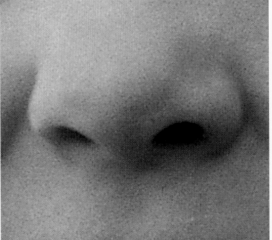

All my
parts will
grow and
grow

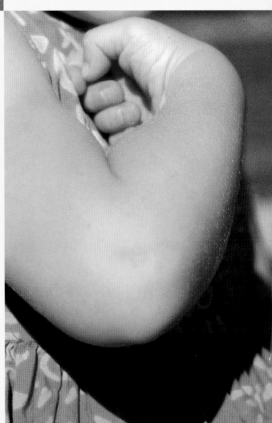

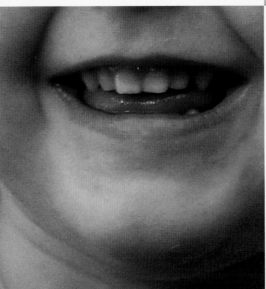

Finger, toe, elbow, knee

This is my BODY,
look at me!

For Emily—
An important part of my life.

First published in the United States of America in 2001 by
Walker Publishing Company, Inc.

Published simultaneously in Canada by Fitzhenry and Whiteside,
Markham, Ontario L3R 4T8

Library of Congress Cataloging-in-Publication Data
Rotner, Shelley.
Parts / Shelley Rotner.
p. cm.
Summary: Rhyming text and close-up photographs
provide clues for the identity of larger everyday objects.
ISBN 0-8027-8753-3 (hc.) ·· ISBN 0-8027-8754-1
[1. Visual perception. 2. Stories in rhyme.] I. Title.

PZ8.3.R755 Par 2001
[E]··dc21   00-046283

Printed in Hong Kong

2 4 6 8 10 9 7 5 3 1

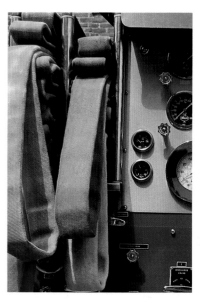